Summa

of

The Biggest Bluff by Maria Konnikova

How I Learned to Pay Attention, Master Myself, and Win

Spark Reads

Note to readers:

This is an unofficial summary & analysis of Maria Konnikova's "The Biggest Bluff" designed to enrich your reading experience. Buy the original book here.

My Free Gift To You

As A Way to Say "Thank You" For Being a Fan of Our Series, I've included a Free Gift for You: A report on How to Lead in All Aspects of Your Life. For You, Free.

If you'd like one, please visit:

https://sparkreads.clickfunnels.com/pg-freegift

The Spark Reads Team

Table of Contents

SUMMARY OVERVIEW

This summary presents a step by step account of the journey the author took to learn how to tame luck. It narrates how her curiosity, motivated by her experiences of bad luck, led her to discover poker as the ideal game to understand better how she could overcome her misfortunes (bad luck). "Could she really tame luck?" This is the question that you will answer upon completion of this summary.

The summary provides a unique perspective on how playing poker can unravel the mysteries of life where chance and skill determine how your life plays out. It also acknowledges the role of true mentorship by Erik Siedel, a Poker Hall of Fame inductee with millions of earnings, who offered guidance to the author to transition from a novice to a pro poker player. You will learn the lessons typical of an amateur's pitfalls, the in-between lessons at the intermediate level, and her viewpoint upon achieving proficiency. The author will get to share with you her experiences of both defeat and triumph through her adventure. You will get to learn how her new pursuit accorded her epiphanies about life, which are eye-opening and applicable to life.

Therefore, this summary is a vault of the incredible lessons that Maria Konnikova amassed through her quest. The Biggest Bluff is not the *how-to* guide of playing poker, but its insight provides direction on how to maximize your skills in life to flourish even when luck may not work in your favor.

PRELUDE: Las Vegas, July 2017

There is no better way to match the lesson contained in this section than, to begin with an epigraph that the author, Maria Konnikova, uses to outline the theme of her book. As Thomas Pynchon's Fausto Maijstral asserts, *"Life's single lesson: that there is more accident to it than a man can ever admit to in a lifetime and stay sane."* In other words, it is hard for a man to appreciate the degree of randomness in life, for if he acknowledged that life is random, the realization would be maddening.

The author demonstrates a fundamental lesson in life that any human being has experienced at one point in his or her life.

It starts with the author describing the mood and atmosphere of one of the grandest Poker tournaments in 2017. It was the *Main Event* for the World Series of Poker (WSOP); it was, in many ways, the *"World cup, the Masters, the Super-Bowl"* in the world of poker. A win at this event automatically meant that you had to go into the annals of poker history.

In her case, she had prepared for this event countless times and raised the $10,000 as buy-in. She reveals that she got into poker to understand better how *"skill"* and *"luck"* played out and in the process, learn what she could control and what was beyond her control. While she was meant to be playing poker at the *Main Event*, she became sick. At that point, Maria was barfing in a bathroom at the Rio Hotel and Casino. The author wasn't sure of what caused her discomfort. Whether it was food poisoning, stomach flu, or just a terrible reaction to stress, it rendered it impossible for her to play her chips. As the author records that she had taken *Advil* to prevent her migraine, performed *Yoga* to relax her body that morning and even slept for nine hours. Despite all the preparation, she still ended up being absent at the table with her chips dwindling in numbers for every poker round that elapsed. One would be stupid to spend a ridiculous amount of money to enter a tournament and not play. Summarily, the migraine kept her away.

Maria starts to learn her lesson about life even before starting to play. She notes that in life, there are things that can't be *"controlled"*. She admitted that "No one can predict or calculate for *"dumb bad luck"*- one can plan, but the outcome will prevail as it should. She learns that she could try her best, but anything else was not up to her to determine. Her reasons for not being at the poker table did not matter. She had no one to direct her complaints. As a lesson, the author learns that one can't *"bluff"* chance. She even acknowledges the phrase, *"Man plans, God laughs."*

CHAPTER ONE – ANTE UP: New York, Later Summer 2016

"Are you curious to find out what motivated the author to start playing poker?" In a nutshell, we can say that the events in her life, coupled with her curiosity, played an active role. "What happens when bad things happen and you simply don't have the answers to why you keep on experiencing streaks of bad luck?" In Maria's case, her mom lost her job and her tough grandma who had survived World War II, Stalin, Khrushchev, and even Gorbachev slipped on the floor and died. Her husband also lost his job, and the startup he had planned to join, never started.

To make matters worse, the author was diagnosed with an autoimmune disease that made her allergic to almost everything. Her condition was idiopathic and. If you were in her shoes, I bet you'd go to great lengths to make meaning of all that was happening, not only to her but also to her family members.

Maria knew that she had done well with herself, but as a believer in the idea that life was *"random"*, she had to investigate which among, *"skill"* or *"chance"*, was primarily responsible for getting her to the level she was in life. That is how she ended up trying to understand the role *"fate"* had played in her life and what portion could be ascribed to her *"own doing"*. "What portion of your life is owed purely to *"stupid luck"*?" and "What share of it can be credited to your *"efforts"*?" As you ponder the answers to those questions, don't forget that Maria was in the same boat as you. She was determined to make s distinction between what was *"random"* and what was *"intentional"* in her life.

Perhaps another example to show you how she had always been intrigued by the relationship between *"skill"* and *"chance"* was her Ph.D. research. She developed a simulated stock market game that tested decision-making skills under pressure. The study entailed thousands of participants. When playing, each participant hoped to pick *"good"* over *"bad"* stock but also had the option to invest in bonds. The game would eventually answer questions such as "How often are you in actual control of a situation?" or, if luck was involved, "How would your perception of being in control affect your decision making?" Additionally, "How would you respond to a situation of uncertainty having incomplete information?"

What we can learn from the results of her experiment is typical of how we respond to the events in life. We usually overestimate the degree of control that we have over life. We think that our skill is *"superior"* to luck, and because of this overestimation, we end up making decisions that are not optimal. "Did you know that once we become overconfident, we fail to learn because the essential information relayed to us by the environment becomes diminished?" As Maria described, it was difficult for the overconfident players to switch to winning stocks or even make a go at the bonds. "Are you the overconfident player who refuses to learn how to achieve *"real control"* over your environment?" Remember that the *"illusion of control"* will prevent you from gaining *"real control"*. The environment knows more than you do. "Is it true that we are fond of ignoring the less desirable messages communicated to us by the environment?" If you fail to heed the message that the environment conveys to you, you'll outrightly lose. The unpleasant truth from her study was that even when under the control of the rule of chance, we often think that we are still in control.

Although her research was eye-opening, it did not provide her the answers she was looking for. She still had questions about the role of *"luck"* and *"skill"* in her life. "How could she best apply theoretical knowledge to promote better decision making?"

Another insightful section in the chapter is when the author discusses the equation of *"skill"* and *"luck"* concerning the human mind. "Why is it difficult for one to appreciate probabilities?" We don't understand *"skill"* and *"luck"* because they are probabilistic, and our minds are non-probabilistic. According to the author, while our minds are intuitive, statistics (probabilities) are counterintuitive. "What can you learn from this?" It is the fact that we do not internalize the rules of numeric, or in summary, we rarely takes statistical data with the seriousness it deserves. Instead, we rely heavily on our own *"gut feelings"* or *"intuition"*.

"What is the one way that can cause you to have a change of mind?" You cannot deny that people trust their own experiences over what data from research has shown. Our reactions are never in line with statistics. Only when we have personally undergone through experience or know of someone who has experienced a similar event can we then be able to change our minds. Statistics may report that the chances of slipping on the bathroom floor are higher than that of experiencing a terrorist attack. Try convincing a person who survived 9/11 even with such data. I bet it would be an exercise in futility.

Maria warns that our faiths in our experiences are mostly *"skewed"* as they don't serve as the best teachers.

"Where did the author get her motivation to play poker?" I hope you have not forgotten about the unfortunate incidents in her life. It is natural to notice when bad things are happening to you. Maria did, and she desperately searched for answers. At this point, she chanced upon a book, *"Theory of Games and Economic Behaviour"* by Jon Von Neumann. He was a remarkable scientist and dubbed the *"Father of Game Theory"*. A strong advocate of Poker, he championed for it as integral in solving *"life's greatest decision challenges"*. It was the only card game that presented a balance between *"skill"* and *"chance"*. To just show how this was the case, poker did not present the uncertainty (pure chance) of the Roulette wheel, neither the certainty of chess due to its information and mathematical elegance.

After being convinced by Von Neumann's rationale, this is how the author picked poker as the ideal game to investigate *"skill"* and *"chance"*. It was practical and experimental. It was the perfect representation of how the human mind works when learning. It entailed a *"systematic process"* and not a *"one-off event"*. She settled on the "No Limit Texas Hold'em" variation of poker. It featured a strong emotional attachment due to the high risk and high reward involved. "Could poker give her the answers that she sought? Could it give her clarity of direction in her healing journey or even maximize her wins when planning for her career?" I know you are equally marveled and can't resist thinking whether poker can do the same for you.

Upon deciding, the last section of the chapter describes her interaction with Erik Siedel and how he agreed to be her coach. Erik revealed to her that her background in psychology would be imperative in her new journey of learning poker. "What unique skills or training are you bringing to the table that can give you an edge?" Maria concludes with the message that her book is not about how to *"play poker"* but how to *"play the world"*.

CHAPTER TWO – THE BIRTH OF A GAMBLER: Boston, fall 2016

"Is it true that most people regard poker as *"gambling"*?" As long as people have the wrong perspective about anything that you do, be sure you'll receive criticism. The author was no exception when she expressed her desire to learn poker to her family. Her grandma, Anya, was particularly critical of her decision for she associated poker with *"gambling*." I guess your viewpoint when compared to other people, will always matter. When they saw poker as "*gambling*," Maria was aware that it would be a daunting task to convince people that poker was an ideal tool for teaching decision making. "What happens when people are skeptical about an idea that you are convinced about?" You do not give up but take it up as a challenge. That was exactly what she did. According to her, games like baccarat or craps were *"truly"* gambling, but poker was a game of chance, just like football or basketball, where an injury can abruptly end your career. Think about the games you've played, "Did they incorporate elements of chance?" If they did, "Can you admit that you were *"gambling"* when you participated in such sporting activities?" Daniel Kahneman even said that *"luck"* was behind most successful investment funds as the stock selection is a game of chance.

"What is the difference between poker and chess?" According to the author, in poker, the best hands can lose, and the worst hands can win. It is different from games of perfect information-like chess where, to win, you had no option but to be the best. "Why do you think poker players are highly respected?" The answer lies in the fact that you have to possess superior skills in *"every human sense"* to win in a game of poker. According to the author, a successful poker player is likely to have a higher skill level than others in professions such as investing, which are respectable.

Interestingly, unlike in life, poker is different from gambling because the *"illusion of skill"* is eliminated through an immediate feedback mechanism.

"Is betting a good thing?" Perhaps this question can be confusing, and you might think of it as a *bête noire* unless you harbor a rational mind. Maria notes that betting represents an effective way of overcoming the drawbacks of our decision-making processes. She goes a step further to divulge that the superiority of poker lies in *"betting*." Now, you wonder, "How so?"

Immanuel Kant, the German philosopher, believed that betting was the *"cure of false confidence,"* which arose out of ignorance of the world's probabilistic nature. Without betting in poker, probabilistic thinking would be hard to grapple with as it is *"integral"* to the learning process. It is indisputable that your brain will learn best when you have placed a stake.

Kant gave the example of a doctor who had already diagnosed a disease, although his decision was *"not necessarily correct."* "If the doctor were to bet on his diagnosis, would he be as sure as the first time he made the decision?" The reality is that the doctor would pause and re-evaluate. This time around, the doctor would entertain the possibility that he might have *"been wrong."*

You may have been a Hillary Clinton supporter during the 2016 presidential elections. She had a

71% chance of being declared the winner compared to Trump's 21%. If you were to put a stake (bet) on the outcome, "Would you bet with the same certainty? Would you place your money on Clinton?" It is highly likely that the second time around, you'll be able to see that a margin of error exists, and it is therefore not as *"certain"* as before. The second time around, the 71% would not seem like the 100% sure win you envisaged in the first round. You can thus clearly see that betting gives us the benefit of analyzing our decisions in deep scrutiny.

"Is there any benefit to learning the importance of probabilities through our experiences?" Maria is quick to point out that if we don't cherish probabilities, we all risk suffering losses. It is no secret that once you bet the wrong amount, a painful loss will always ensue. The author warns that you are likely to lose money if you say, *"I think I'm good here"* without an actual quantification of the number of times you actually felt *"good"*. True to life, humans frequently disregard statistics and embrace something only because it seems right. "How often do you find yourself in such a situation, buying something without thinking because it sounded right to you or because somebody else said it was *"good"*?"

"Do you trust in luck?" Well, if you do, then know that it is a *"losing enterprise"*. Even with the knowledge of probabilities, Girolamo Cardano, the inventor of Primero – the earliest form of poker, insisted that *"luck"* could not be tamed. The only *"certain"* (sure way) to guarantee a win to him was by *"cheating"*. In conclusion, Maria discovered poker to be a *"skilled endeavor"* and that she alone, not anybody else, could determine how to play and suffer the consequences of her actions. That motivated her.

CHAPTER THREE – THE ART OF LOSING: New York, fall 2017

This chapter delves into the subject of *"failure"* and why it is vital in promoting learning.

You can only advance onto the next level if you have mastered your current level. In this chapter, Maria had gotten a commendable grasp of the fundamentals of poker theory. Erik recommended that she would then advance to playing poker online using real money but for tiny stakes. After enough practice at online poker, Erik would allow her to play real-life poker in real casinos. "What can you notice about Erik's strategy?" With such a plan, it would be easier for her to make slow but sure progress until she got to the bigger tournaments. It teaches you that to be good at anything, you must appreciate the learning processes.

The lessons that Erik teaches her are crucial. From them, you can quickly see why playing poker can help improve your decision making in life. Maria is taught how to use cards to exploit her weak opponents and learns the type of poker players -

"aggressive" and *"super aggressive"*. You will be impressed to find out that even the worst hands are still playable given the right circumstances. "Did you know that a stack size in poker is critical?" As a matter of fact, according to Erik, you can calculate your position by calculating your risk of becoming broke. Another great counsel by Erik is how a two-hundred-dollar tournament and a hundred-thousand-dollar tournament demanded different playing styles for anyone to win.

Another takeaway from this chapter is to embrace failure. Remember that Maria was an amateur and trying her best to learn poker. According to her coach, *failure* is the best teacher. "How will you know that you are good at something when all you do is win?" You can agree that only when you are losing do you get to determine if you have grit for it. In her case, Maria was warned that there was no way that she could become good at poker by getting lucky.

"What do you do when things don't go according to plan?" Such moments are the best as you get to discover yourself better. Erik describes this as the moment of *"conquering"* yourself. To him, you only become a winner when you have suffered defeat because failure will give you*"objectivity"* that success can't provide. I'm sure if you just keep winning from the onset, you won't confidently tell whether your success was the result of your brilliance or just a streak of luck. Starting with success can make you develop *"illusions of control"* in the event of pure chance. Don't forget that when learning, failure (disaster) is your best *"teacher"* because it creates a room for objectivity while success may be treated as an *"enemy"*. Though the two arise out of chance, disaster is regarded the *"better"* teacher as it the perfect antidote for *"overconfidence"*.

Objectivity is devoid of emotions and allows you to ask yourself if you are thinking correctly or understand the basics. That is the foremost critical step, Erik told her. You need to look at things from a *business* perspective and refrain from taking things *personally*. If you are not objective when playing any game, you will lose. Without an objective evaluation of your life, you are likely going to make the wrong decisions. Remember that just like in poker, when it comes to your life, a good ability of self-assessment (impartial) coupled with critical thinking are consequential.

"When is the best time for you to quit? Is it when your career is plunging or when you are at the pinnacle?" In painting the significance of objectivity and critical thinking, as an example, Erik quit playing competitive poker when he was at the top of his game. He had won $1.63million, but when he subjected himself to an unbiased self-assessment, he found out that he had gotten older and weaker against the opposition in the field that grew stronger with time.

The first real lesson of the author in poker was about *"losing"* and not winning. "Can you lose and remain objective about your chances of winning?" If you answered in the affirmative, "How can you then apply this lesson in life?" For a start, no loss is easy. As the poker master put it, you can lose and make a comeback in life, and any loss in the process will not be viewed as a personal failure. Erik lost his job in the crush of 1987 while his wife was pregnant but never took it personally. According to the author, his uniqueness was his ability to remain *"objective"* to himself and his level of play while being egoless. "What do you do when you suffer a loss? Do you learn from your losses?"

Towards the end of the chapter, another critical lesson was served - Erik calls for Maria to be *"open-minded"* and inquisitive by *"questioning more"*. Should *"less certainty"* translate to *"more inquiry"*? The answer is yes, according to Maria - when you don't receive any concrete advice or get any real answers, you need to challenge yourself to think it through. This way, you will find your answers. Erik didn't give her all the answers because he wanted her to find out for herself. In the end, she learns that critical thinking was key to making good decisions in poker, a game that was riddled with *"uncertainty"*.

CHAPTER FOUR – THE MIND OF A STRATEGIST: New York, Late Fall 2016

This chapter bases on the events of online gameplay and focuses on the author's mistakes. Through the help of her coach, she learns about the various strategies she could have adopted concerning specific situations of play.

I bet that we all would be very successful if we knew exactly what cards to play, given that we knew the specific or the right circumstances to play them. To be able to do this, you must practice until you become proficient. "Do you believe in the ten-thousand-hour rule?" It is clear that Maria does not believe in the rule when she refers to exceptions owing to "*aptitude, genes* or *determination*" as having an upper hand. To her, you did not need to practice for ten thousand hours to become a master. As she put it, *"practice"* was critical, and she was going to do just that to improve her skills in poker.

Determination is no doubt one of the ingredients of success. In the chapter, this was demonstrated when the author had to cross over from her home state, New York, to New Jersey, which had legalized online poker.

Some people get ahead in life by exploiting the loopholes that exist. As part of her psychological strategy, the author chose the name *"psychic"* and used an avatar of a dachshund puppy. She had learned that poker was a man's world and that they played against *"real"* people differently from how they played against *"girls"*. She was even conscious of statistics reporting that the players with a female avatar were bluffed six percent more by the male players. "How are you taking advantage of the loopholes that you've identified?"

We learn best through our mistakes. When we take the time to study our mistakes, we develop better strategies at dealing with similar scenarios in the future. Erik watched a recorded version of the online gameplay and analyzed the decisions Maria had taken. Being a good coach, he did not hesitate to correct her. One such lesson is the fact that *"position is king"*. In the poker table, what this means is that one should not be in a hurry to decide until *"enough information"* is availed. In poker, when you are the last person to play, you benefit from incorporating information from players who played before you. That will promote better decision making when it is your turn to play.

"Why is it proper for you to reflect before making your move?" Thinking, according to Erik, sets apart *"mindless activity"* from *"mindful activity"*. You must encourage a clear thought process to dictate your next move even when you are in a high-pressure situation where an urgent decision must be made. Thinking in poker can help you determine the right *"bet sizing"* by evaluating risk, frequency, and betting size.

Playing poker, she discovered it was like a military campaign where she was the army commander. And any military action will be motivated by the situational analysis and the make-up of the territory. It will be easy for you to know whether your success is borne out of *"skill"* or *"luck"* because, in a military campaign, there must be a plan, a process, a system, and a feedback mechanism.

If you are fully aware of the power of your position, you can decide a course of action that will guarantee you success. "Is timing also crucial?" If you play too early, your advantage will decline, and you can be attacked from multiple angles. Even in such a scenario, Erik insists that *"thinking"* of all possible permutations would be key.

Perhaps determining what will be accomplished by what *"tactic"* and if a more affordable option existed to achieve the same outcome, is applicable in life. "Have you ever paused to consider how you could attain a particular goal using the least available resources?"

In creating the mind of a strategist, the *"perception of an image"* is discussed. I guess many people would want to portray a particular image so that they don't appear weak. The author was in much a similar debacle. She did not want to appear weak, so she played aggressively. According to Erik's advice, you are reminded not to care about what other people think about you. As a good commander, you are allowed to mold an image only if it is strategically aimed at future action.

The author also reveals how our unique gifts can devour our opponents. "Did you know that the dragonfly is an effective predator compared to the likes of the lion and the cheetah?" A 2012 Harvard University research shows that the dragonfly boasts a prey-capture rate of 95 percent, far above that of a lion and the cheetah. If you could watch your prey and predict its next action and then device an appropriate action, you will annihilate it. The author likened Erik to a dragonfly. His deep and detailed analysis of opponents, with his disposition to do anything in light of the circumstances at play, made him a winner of €2million at the EPT Grand Super High Roller Final against Dzmitry Urbanovich.

"Are you keen to observe the analogy that you give to the things that you interact with in life?" When Maria approached poker like *"war"*, Erik thought of it as a *"jazz band"* with him as a member of the band. "Do you agree that his analogy was better than that of the author?" When hers was *"zero-sum"* involving causalities, Erik's entailed building a connection and maintaining synchronization i.e.*"positive-sum"*. "Do you think that how you view an engagement affects the quality of your performance?"

Maria demonstrated the importance of learning from our mistakes to improve our skills. She used all that she learned from Erik and went on to win an online tournament. She described how the skills she acquired with poker were valuable when she was able to negotiate for better payment rates for a magazine article. She admitted that in the past, she would have accepted lower pay than what she got. As you contemplate your life, "What lessons from a game you love are you applying in your life?"

CHAPTER FIVE – A MAN'S WORLD: New York, winter 2016

There isn't a better way to commence this chapter than by stating the first seven words of a quote by David Mamet. His quote straightforwardly reads, *"Playing poker is also a masculine ritual..."* This chapter provides a window into the role of women in the game of poker from the author's personal view. It touches on the perception of women and the barriers that exist for them to thrive in the game. You will also get a few pointers on why people make certain decisions.

If you are like Maria, interested in learning poker, "What do you do when you are told that the *"The poker environment is unfriendly to women"*? When you are told that as a woman, you have to be in a class of your own, extremely brilliant like Liv Boeree and Vanessa Selbst?" It didn't take long for her to realize that poker to women was a *"harsh environment"*. For women, it demanded a level of smarts that would, by any standard, be *"exceptional"*. She observes that few women came to play poker, but the majority came to *"socialize"*.

The chapter describes how her coach wanted the author to boost her *"aggression"*. He had noticed that she was not playing aggressively when this style of play was mostly desired. It meant that she couldn't capitalize on great opportunities. In one charity event, she thought she would just accompany Erik, only to find out that he had organized for her to play at the event. She was unprepared, but Erik thought it would provide her with excellent practice in readiness for Las Vegas. It would be the first live poker game for her, and in the process, she gained a perspective on the position of women in the poker world.

Maria was advised that her *"image as a woman"* could be invaluable. When playing against men in a live event, the fact that she was *"female"* would offer her some degree of anonymity, which she could utilize. You see, men will be alerted at every crazy move she made, causing them to fold because they thought that she was incapable of such a move.

Are there times in life we know what we should do, but we still take pleasure in the comfort zone that we are in because of a flawed perception of security?" If you ever felt this way at one point, you can relate to Maria's situation. She knew that she needed to play aggressively to improve her skills, but her passiveness persisted and was losing her poker chips. The tough question in her mind was, "Why wasn't she revving up her aggression?" Upon introspection, she discovered that *"social conditioning"* was to blame for her inability to be aggressive. The author pondered over the biases leveled against women in society. She added that aggression in men speaks of their potential, but it would be interpreted in a bad light in women. A realization that the author made is that *"women have been socialized into passivity"*. She learned that she had not yet triumphed over socialization despite her education and professional achievements. "Why are women few in poker?" In a profound discovery, the author reveals that the biases that women have had to fight are represented by a massive scale in an environment where men make up 97% of the population.

"Why is it so hard to learn a new skill?" Sometimes you might think that you are starting from a *"new slate"* only to discover that you have *"baggage"*, and your slate is therefore not new. The author attributed her reluctance to play aggressively to the *"emotional baggage"* she had unwittingly accumulated throughout her professional life.

Being thrown into a live game of poker presented her with challenges she never before experienced. It was tough for her to hide her struggles as playing live meant that she was *"exposed"*. We all make mistakes in a new environment because of fear. She did make mistakes when she played, but she could understand the context of her play, and her courage grew slowly. Just like in life, when you are thrown into a strange place, you need to doggy-paddle until, at some point, you can swim comfortably with ease. She was happy that she could think through her decisions. That was an improvement on her side.

In her plays, she won and almost convinced herself that she had a hot hand. It is the perception that if a player who played well had *"hot"* hands, the player would continue playing well. She lost afterward. The author talked of *"Gambler's fallacy"*. That is when you lose, and instead of quitting, you continue playing because you believe you will start winning at some point. It is true that probabilities acquire abnormal distribution tendencies. It is natural for human beings to want probabilities to be distributed normally so that they can believe that since you have suffered a streak of bad runs, the good ones should follow. Life is a game of chances, a game of probabilities, and what you expect to happen might never happen. According to Frank Lantz, a game designer, one of the *"idiosyncrasy of game design"* is the jiggered probabilities in modern video games so that people don't label the setup as being "*rigged*". Frank referred to poker as the *"best game"* because it isn't the product of a game designer in modern thinking. Poker, to him, does not twitch probabilities to accommodate misconceptions.

"Why do smart people continue to make the same decisions when the runs are in their favor?" Simple, they believe in *"luck"* and want the good run to persist indefinitely while wanting to believe that a bad streak is ancient history.

People also have the *"illusion of luck"*, which Psychologist Julian Rotter in 1966 explained using a concept she called the *"locus of control"*. You are classified as having *either an external or internal* locus of control. If you hold the view that events will play out as they should and you have little control over them, then you have an *"external locus of control"*. If you believe that you affect the outcomes, usually way more than is the case, you have an *"internal locus"*. A lackadaisical attitude towards work and mental depression is common with those harboring an external locus of control while those with an internal locus of control are healthier mentally.

"How then is it possible for us to deal with uncertainty as illustrated by the law of probabilities?" The author answers this debacle by saying that your distaste for bad luck needs to be cured and the exuberance associated with your good runs have to be tamed.

CHAPTER SIXTH – NO BAD BEATS: Las Vegas, Winter 2017

This chapter describes Maria's first-time experience in Las Vegas and how the glitz of Vegas dazzled her. She accompanied Erik to familiarize herself with the *"real"* Vegas experience. She has to play poker tournaments, which will help her improve.

This is one of the chapters where good mentorship from Erik plays a critical role in shaping Maria into a skilled player. The crash course on *"Poker economics"* was effective enough to convince Maria to pick those tournaments with lower stakes over those she had initially picked. Erik encouraged her to play at places with many affordable buy-ins of between $(40-60) and not those of $140 and above.

One such lesson from "poker economics" is *"bankroll"* - money is set aside specifically for poker and not any other business. Maria had never heard of it and learned from Erik. We can learn the importance of setting aside a dedicated amount of money for specific projects. Maria was advised by Erik to have a separate account for her poker engagements and not draw the money from her monthly expenses account.

"How important is risk mitigation?" In life, many people find it hard to protect themselves against risks. Erik reiterated that people should always budget for the bad times. "How many players earn millions only to spend them wastefully?" There are many, and I know you've read many stories about them. If you are not prepared for the worst, which will come at some point, you'll never recover even if you are a talented player. The author reveals that "Skills don't matter when you lack a safety net."

Erik's strategy was realistic, practical, and that he prioritized on minimizing risk. He picked out the Golden Nugget, an old casino in old-school Vegas, for the *"real"* feeling of Vegas. He also wanted her to participate in the WSOP ladies' event. To him, this type of event would be a *"safe bet"* for her. Though unhappy for she did not desire to participate in the softest of all the WSOP events, she was apprised that only 23 females out of 1503 wins could be attributed to women in its history.

One thing to note is that when she went in to play, Maria was determined to master the game and to be known as a *"good"* player and not a *"good female"* player at poker.

It is while playing that she got to learn that, *"Appearances can be deceiving."* "Have you ever experienced a zero-sum landscape?" In such an environment, an opponent takes advantage of others, uses underhand tactics, or uses the old angle. Maria encountered one such guy who, like a *"Fox"*, preyed on weaker victims. In her mind, she called him *"Mr. Fox"*. When he played at the table, he pretended to be a newbie at poker but still went on to amass a large stack of chips the way a *"pro"* would. "Do you know of such people in your life?" Those whom you trusted only to get stabbed in the back or when you discovered that your so-called *"friend"* had used you.

"Do you remember the time that you almost got lucky?" This section of the chapter will offer you critical insight into why the habit of *"almost"* should be discouraged. Maria had reported to Erik how she almost won using a set of nines. In poker, this is referred to as *"bad beats"*. Erik found this habit distasteful. According to him, focusing on the bad beats never improved a player. Her eyes should not be fixed on the *"luck"* but the *"process"*. She learned of how thinking and emotional states are affected by how we frame things. Thinking about bad beats can have drastic consequences on the state of our wholeness. Seeing yourself as a victim or a victor based on your experiences is instrumental to your wellness. Entertaining bad beats cause you to wallow in misfortune, and at those moments, you cannot identify opportunities or take actions that can make you better. As she learned, by being a *"seed of resilience"*, you become a *"luck amplifier"* and make it easier for other people to help you. Someone will remind you of a job opportunity because of your positive attitude. Even when you are being dealt with heavy blows by life, this attitude will make you feel happier, well-adjusted, and ready for the times that variance will be on your side.

"What do you do when you experience bad beats?" According to Erik, the best players don't let bad beats drag them down. They know that they need to have a positive mindset even when facing *"dead* cards". Just like in life, poker is a game of perception; once your opponents read *"defeat"* on your face, they will trump over you without hesitation. Her coach counseled her to just focus on what was *"controllable"* i.e. her *"decision making"* and not on the cards that she couldn't *"control"*. He and Maria agreed never to talk about bad beats again.

CHAPTER SEVEN – TEXTING YOUR WAY OUT OF MILLIONS: Las Vegas, Winter 2017

The chapter focuses on the uniqueness of poker, the essentials of paying attention, not only in poker but in everything that you do, and finally on the perception of loss.

Maria has tagged along her coach to acquire more insights for her learning by watching Erik play with other poker players.

A *"motley bunch"* is how she described the poker players. The variety could best be expressed by players who hailed from different backgrounds. It didn't matter whether you grew up with wealth or not. Whether you went to Brown, taught at Harvard, or merely a high school dropout. Whether raised by a single parent or both, it still didn't matter. At the poker table, anyone can participate for as long as you managed the buy-in. Annoying habits or foul social skills go unpenalized. Unlike many other sports, it does not discriminate based on your genes, height, or muscle endowment. It comes close to the actual *"meritocracy"*— only your skill matters. Even women are welcome to display their worth. The blind and the deaf can still play. "What lesson did she take away from her observation?" Inclusivity was the lesson that the author learned regarding the game of poker.

Imagine starting as a beginner, as the author reports, a variance can work for or against you. She undoubtedly was dedicated to getting the best wisdom from the best. One such lesson that forms the pillar of the chapter is that of *"paying attention"*. When playing, Erik would let her see his cards so that she could read the play. Cary Katz referred to Erik as the *"Silent Assassin"* after he lost the pot to him. "How did he achieve that?" Only by *"paying attention"* will your focus be rewarded. With all the activities going on at the table, it was overwhelming for her to learn. However, Erik revealed to her that by paying attention, one could pick up tells and betting patterns even in the presence of *"attention grabbers"*. "How many times have you lost out because you were not attentive to the essential information?" I'm sure we've all experienced it at some point. To make it worse,

Maria learned that even the pro players suffered from a similar malady. Some of them kept looking at their phones, and others looked at sports news that was unrelated. Your phone can be a distraction, your T.V. can be a distraction, and without focus, consequences follow.

One of the great examples of focus is a player called LuckyChewy. Erik had instructed Maria to watch him closely. He was unique from the rest, with a perfect posture, and even and intense gaze capable of accommodating the entire room. To her, LuckyChewy seemed like the *"incarnation of focus"*. His focus paid when he was able to avoid a loss when playing against a player named Bob. His observations led to him make a great decision. On the other hand, Edward was always distracted and depended much on an algorithm, a program that would help him decide his next move. He continued when Chewy folded. His confidence was in the information he received from the program. It made him overconfident, but extra information does not translate to *"certainty"*. Edward went on to face a major loss. Overconfidence can best be mitigated by *"attention"*. Paying attention sharpens your skill edge, and bad beats can even be avoided. "How many times in your life were you careful to read the danger signals that warned you of imminent danger, and yet you chose to ignore them?"

If observation becomes a priority, then chance will always favor the prepared mind. "Why do you refer to some people as the lucky ones?" As the author expressed, they are not lucky because the *good* stuff is happening to them, but it is because they are *alert* and, therefore, aware of them when they happen. Although variance will remain *uncontrolled*, we can still *control* our attention and exploit it.

Chewy finished second owing to his presence in the game. After the game, the author interviewed him and learned about his secret - the *"element of flow,"* an idea of the free flow of body motion that perfectly syncs with the previous move. He learned it from practicing *Yoga, Kung fu*, and *Tai Chi*. To Chewy, a winner in poker is one who can apply pressure in the correct amount and also concede retreat in the right amount.

The author also discovered that Chewy was Zennish when it came to embracing loss. To him, *"loss is the way of learning to win"*. He views it in the cosmic sense. A loss to him means that another event has to occur for him to be channeled to success. Chewy reminded Maria that "In the overall scheme of life, there is no aboard for negative emotions." A lesson that can be drawn from this, "Pay attention" and "Never over-invest your emotions in your sadness or misfortune."

CHAPTER EIGHT – A STORYTELLING BUSINESS: Las Vegas, March 2017

This chapter depicts another great lesson that the author picks up after interacting with Phil Galfond, another poker genius.

Sometimes your outlook can easily influence the rate of your progress when it comes to learning. Phil offers her a piece of advice that will change the way she views poker. *"Poker is storytelling"* and adds that it is a *"narrative puzzle"* where the pieces must be put together to fit.

When teaching her how to gain competency in poker, you get to learn that each way had its merit(s) and demerit(s). For example, Phil tells her that learning by *rote* was great for immediate results, but when an unforeseen circumstance emerges, dealing with it would be difficult. In other words, although you have the competency, you will lack *mastery*. "Are there instances in your life where you thought you knew it all, then suddenly, something happened, and you didn't know how to tackle it?"

Phil explains to her that cramming and memorizing concepts are profitable in the short term. *Critical thinking*, he insisted, would be crucial even in unpredictable situations. He reminded her that in poker, she should be a *detective* and a *storyteller*. That involved reading the actions of an opponent to know what those actions *meant* and what they *did not mean*. They discussed the *"omission neglect"* where people pay attention when a dog barks, but they fail to do so when it doesn't. According to Phil, crucial evidence can be communicated even in the absence of information. In poker, a player should conjecture what the opponent is trying to hide. He reminds her that poker is like constructing a story that will eventually add up. She, therefore, has to think in advance whether her pieces will add up. Also, being aware of the story, her opponent is trying to create so that she can easily pick out areas where their pieces don't add up.

If you don't have a credible reason for doing something, the chances are high that you will fail.

Phil advises her to always look for the *"motivation"*, the *"why"*. He encourages her to ask, "Why she made a particular move?" or "Why her opponent made a specific move?" That she should never judge the actions of other people without discovering their *motivation*. Through his advice, she learns that she is not just an army commander nor a jazz musician, but more than that, she is a *detective* and a *storyteller*.

"What lesson can you learn from the advice given to her by Phil? Have you ever been angry at someone because you thought they acted stupidly? Did you take a step back and asked yourself why they did what they did?

You've heard the saying, *"Practice makes perfect"*. Playing more poker for Maria would help balance her theoretical knowledge of poker and her skills. To Phil, too much knowledge that is not backed with experience is *valueless*. It only bestows you an *illusion of power*. On top of it, there were no shortcuts to learning poker.

The author puts into practice the counsel Phil gave her and combines it with her other experiences. She plays more poker in the ensuing weeks in preparation for the *Main Event*. By applying the lessons, she starts to win at some tournaments. Those first wins, including garnering a *"Hendon score"*, a site that tracks poker tournament winners, reinforce her confidence. These wins remind her that she is making progress. Without them, Maria revealed that she had contemplated giving up. Erik noticed her improvements and encouraged her to try her hand at the European Poker Tournament, which was to be held in Monte Carlo in six weeks.

CHAPTER NINE – THE
GAMBLER AND THE NERD:
Monte Carlo, April 2017

This chapter records the experiences of the author when she finally gets to go to Monte Carlo. It is a whole new ball game for her as she sees herself as an *"international"* poker player.

We can grab some wisdom, especially from realizing that from her tournaments, the author was not playing poker to win but to get the min-cash that is paid out to those poker players who do well in the competition. Erik expressed his concern that her *"cash rate"* was higher than it should be. It was at 50 percent instead of 25 percent. The top is where the real money was, but Maria seemed comfortable aiming for the min-cash. The author admitted that she was afraid of being out of competition with no cash. Erik told her that she could never become a *"winning player"* by playing with a minimum cash mentality.

Despite her wins, Erik also reminded her that Monte Carlo was no Las Vegas. It was expensive, and the high living expenses made her earnings to be less profitable.

Maria's takeaway was for her to get deeper and not confuse her minor victories as a sign that she was doing great. Although they count, her eyes should be on the *bigger prize*. According to the author, many are times that we become complacent because we feel great about *"participation trophies"* instead of attaining a *"podium finish"*. You need to be more ambitious by setting higher targets in your life. Don't just go for a small victory, *"Go in to win it."*

Another critical lesson in this chapter is that on prop bets. It's a type of betting that poker players engage in aside from the actual play. It can be anything from a push-up challenge or a bike ride challenge from Los Angeles to Las Vegas in under two days. The prop bets are meant to push a person to the edge to determine their *"limits of control"*.

In this chapter, the author gets to discuss *Lodden Thinks*, one of the prop bets that she dubbed a *"strange game"*. As Erik explained, the game was created by Antonio Esfandiari and Phil Laak to kick boredom during a poker table that was being televised. The game was about asking a random question, and the third guy would think of an answer, whether right or wrong. The objective was that the person who would get the correct answer or get close to the right answer would win. In the case of Antonio and Phil, Johnny Lodden was the third guy. This game was an instant hit, and it became famous in the world of poker dom. The correct answer to any raised question did not matter. What mattered was what the *third guy* thought as being the *right answer*. To Erik and Maria, *Lodden Thinks* was a game of psychology and perception. It tested how well one can understand the world from the perspective of another person. To win at this game, one has to have a *subjective perception* and be able to tap into it with *good accuracy*. The author gives an example of a game between Doyle Brunson and Phil Ivey with Daniel Negreanu, who played the Lodden. Doyle and Phil had to guess the age of actor Clint Eastwood. Although Doyle won the pot ($8000), Phil beat him at *Lodden Thinks* and earned ($10,000). Not such a bad game after all.

Erik takes the opportunity to warn Maria that knowledge alone about a person (*the Lodden*) without a proper analysis of the *specifics of interaction* can cost you a victory. He gave a personal example where he went on a bet with Antonio Esfandiari while in South Africa. They were to guess the amount of money that Dan Harrington would take to forgo the wearing of socks. Since Dan was a very close friend of Erik, Erik thought that he knew him even better than Dan knew himself. He didn't bother to observe his reactions closely enough i.e. how he behaved in that *"current"* state. He lost one hundred and sixty thousand dollars to Antonio, who was keen enough. Later on, Dan disclosed to Erik that the amount he had guessed was right though, at that moment, Dan's mind had a different figure in mind.

"What can we learn from the example above?" We can learn that there is no perfect model for a human being. We are all subject to changes. Therefore, it is important to make adjustments for specific individuals depending on the *moment* and the *situation at play*. Dan's wrong guess concerning what he believed as preferable, can teach us that a person could be erroneous when it comes to what the mind is telling him or her.

In this chapter, we can learn to appreciate and accommodate people's perceptions of the world. It also reminds us that we are not always right simply because we think we know more about someone. You will notice that such lessons are essential in life and can also be applied in poker when trying to understand how your opponent thinks. To conclude, I'll use a line from the chapter which states, "Like so many things in life, this is a game of people, not hard truths."

CHAPTER TENTH – THE ART OF THE TELL: New York, May 2017

In this chapter, the author admits that her Monte Carlo experience has revealed that she can *"read"* souls. In poker, a *"tell"* is when you can detect the behavioral changes in your opponent and read them as cues that help you evaluate their hands.

You should be careful when trying to read people. Sometimes our implicit biases can get the better of us and cause us to engage in stereotypical actions that lack adequate knowledge (information) to make a good decision. Maria disclosed how she misread an opponent as an *"aggressive maniac"*. That made her plays aggressively and lost her chips in the process.

"Why do you think that in less than thirty-four seconds, you can judge whether somebody is aggressive or trustworthy?" As you observe them longer, your level of confidence based on your judgment surges. As the author points out, this process is the work of your subconscious mind where *"perception"* and not *"thinking"*, that is determined by your logical brain, reign supreme. The subconscious processes it through your visual system.

These *"thin-slice judgments"* as coined by Psychologist Nalini Ambady are decided upon by the expressions and structures given off by the *face*. According to the author, big muscles in men translate to a domineering or an aggressive character. She adds that this type of judgment arises from a *"biased processing"* and not from the point of *"objective reality"*. Maria is quick to warn that *"thin-slice judgments"* fail at the individual level as it is mostly associated with large samples.

The author reveals that when you are told that you chose, for example, an investment adviser due to their friendly nature or you are dating a person because of a jawline, you will vehemently deny that your decisions are snappy. "Do you agree that some of the serious decisions you have made may not have been out of in-depth analysis, but from something as superficial as a *"generous heart"* or a *"fun"* personality?"

The author relays that it is difficult to correct our wrong reads. We are thus susceptible to the same mistakes when a similar situation presents itself in the future. One reason she attributes to this is that we always have excuses instead of accepting that we are the culprits.

In another section, the author says that even after studying con artists in the psychology of deception, spotting a deception is a daunting task, especially if the person is a pro. She dismisses that both the *"eyes"* and the *"face"* cannot be *"good metrics"* for spotting or discerning a deception.

Maria is eager to search for an effective way that can help her better evaluate her opponents. The *Main Event* is only two months away. She is not one to quit and plowed through research to seek an effective strategy to read a person. Through her research, she discovers the works of Michel Slepian, a professor at Columbia, who worked under Ambady on *"psychology of thin-slice judgments"*. The author referred to Slepian's research as *"magical"*. His research on poker players at the WSOP 2009 based on their *"hand motions"* was able to infer the players that had *"goods hands"*. It concluded that the accuracy of picking players who held stronger cards from only reading their hand motions was higher than in those who strictly watched their faces. From the hand motion, they could detect *"fluidity of motion"*, which meant that they had *"confidence"*. It didn't matter to Maria whether adopting this strategy would only boost her edge by a couple of percentages. The knowledge of Slepian's work broadened her intuition. She might have had a *"poker face"* but probably let her guard down in the past in terms of her body language. The author is determined that she would no longer be a *"tell box"* and would pay more attention to her opponents' motions.

CHAPTER ELEVEN – READING MYSELF: New York, May-June 2017

"What if you could read yourself? Do you think knowing yourself better will increase your odds of favorably doing well in the game of life?" This chapter offers insight into the importance of understanding yourself. It is about the author trying her best to improve herself in readiness for the *Main Event*. To do so, she seeks the advice of Blake Eastman. Blake went from psychologist to a poker player and finally turned up as a Behavioral analyst.

Blake was in charge of *"Beyond Tells"* research, which determined the relationship between the "*strength of a hand"* with how a player *"acted"* based on observed patterns. It focused on behaviors and patterns that were *"repeatable"*. The degree of fluidity of motion was an indication of a player's confidence. The research could tell indecisiveness based on how a player held chips. Blake's research went beyond Slepian's work.

Upon her request, Blake studies Maria through much of her live poker plays and uses his research to develop areas where she needed to improve i.e. to become *"locked"* as opposed to being a *"tell"* box.

Blake analyzes her behavior, and they discuss each of his findings.

#1: She rechecks her cards, and Blake warns her that this pattern can be a giveaway. According to him, players with marginal hands often rechecked their cards. #2: She puts her hands on her cards. She is no longer to do so as that can reveal whether she has marginal or top range cards. #3: She starts with commendable consistency, which deviates with time. Her gestures also become dynamic, making it easy for an opponent to read. He warns that the *"Robotic"* approach at the table is the worst as trying to conceal when you are aware often leads to failure. He asks her to allow herself to think before making any actions since the thinking encourages sure moves, which speaks confidence. #4: Maria needs to tone down on her talk and laughter. Any opponent may take advantage and engage her to read her. He also advises her against *"speech play"* in poker. He tells her that there is a high risk of giving out information to an opponent than what she could elicit.

Since the author acknowledges that experience is crucial at picking out *"tells"*, she had to look for a different strategy to somehow make up for her inexperience. Maria talks about how the Cognitive-Affective Personality System (CAPS) is paramount in such a case. CAPS is a model developed by Walter Mischel and Yuichi Shoda to analyze behavior. If you are familiar with CAPS, you will realize that it is the best tool for analyzing behavior in a dynamic environment. According to her, CAPS was the perfect tool since *"People aren't a combination of traits"* but *"a mosaic of reactions to and interactions with situations"*. CAPS was ideal for emotional and psychological dynamics, which emerges best at the poker table. The *"who you are"* comes out best at the poker table as it accords you with all the environment that life can give a person, that of defeat, winning, energy, fatigue, drama, etc.

Another insight to take is that of the *"donkey space"* where a *"donkey"* is the worst of two experts. When deploying the OODA strategy, you can punish the mistakes of your opponent. In the *"donkey space"*, two experts would "constantly Observe, Orient, Decide and Act – OODA" until whoever outmaneuvers the opponent is declared the winner. Maria failed to read the patterns by an opponent, and she found herself the *"donkey"* when playing a major hand.

To the author, getting the right read makes one an exceptional player. She discovers that while it is important to exploit the tells from an opponent, equally paramount is the knowledge that, in turn, your opponent is exploiting you. She realized she was so focused on reading other people that she forgot to read herself. She notes that Blake could tell her how she was revealing physically but couldn't delve into the *"inner psychology"* to understand the motivations behind her actions. She noticed then that she had performed a physical profile but not a psychological profile of herself. She was the first person that she needed to master before trying to master others.

As the chapter concludes, "Can you point out the occasions you hoped that if you had known yourself better, things would have turned out differently?"

CHAPTER TWELVE – FULL TILT: Las Vegas, June-July 2017

This chapter is a continuation of the author's endeavor to improve herself. There is one thing that is truly inspiring about Maria. When she knows that something stands in her way of victory, she will go to the ends of the world to attain the mastery required to obliterate any obstacle that stood in her way. She has to learn fast, for the *Main Event* is only a month away. Upon self-contemplation, she realized that her mind had been fixated on poker to the extent that her *"real"* life has taken a blow. Maria learns the importance of maintaining a balance between *"seeking mastery"* and *"establishing stability"* in her mental and emotional vantage point. "How do you allocate time for yourself and your craft?". No one can argue that *"prowess"* is not an asset when you are not in a state of proper mental health. She needed to recharge but instead went ahead and participated at the preliminaries of WSOP in Vegas. She busted out when she registered a dismal performance simply because she was not mentally and emotionally prepared to compete at that level.

The chapter shows that even after comprehending that she was not ready, she still went ahead and participated in the Main Event, where she only lasted up to the second day before she busted out. "How can you explain her irrational behavior?" *Irrational perseverance* is a concept by Daniel Kahneman in which a person chooses to still engage in an activity even when they know its *irrational*. It has to do with *"planning fallacy"* when we avoid agreeing with the realistic scenario, and instead, we hold on to optimistic timelines that are unrealistic. "How many times have you set a three-month goal deadline only to realize that you need a year to accomplish?" Another reason was the *"sunk cost fallacy"*, which means she only participated because she had invested in the buy-in amount for the tournament. In hindsight, she learned that the art of *"letting go"* when there is a shift in the landscape is potent. "Have you held to something tightly in the past even when its appeal was long gone?" She gives the example of staying in a relationship even when the uncommon is more than the common, or lingering in a *"great"* job where promotions are passed over you. That is typical of our everyday living, and the author warns against this. Learn to let go.

Her situation can also be explained by the perspective of Amos Tversky, who said that a person can still exhibit *"bias"* even when he or she is aware of it. She knew of her fallacy but still tricked herself into believing that participating at the *Main Event* was a *good* idea. "See how you feel in the morning?" Erik had always advised her not to do anything if she didn't feel like doing.

After ignoring all the signs, it came to the point where panic, coupled with overconfidence, led her to make the wrong decisions that Erik had warned her not to make. She failed in the competition.

A couple of months later, the author met Jared Tendler, a psychologist, and a mental health coach. As a psychologist herself, she did not need another psychologist to assess her. She knew that her decision making had to improve, and Jared was the person to help her out. He introduced the concept of identifying the flaws that lay deeper and how the triggers could be removed. Doing so avoids emotional responses that promote faulty judgments. His concept was known as *"Tilt"* and involved the idea that we allow decision making to be interfered with by incidental little emotions, which were not central to the decision process. That, he insisted, curtails rational thinking. Jared guided her to overcome her fears, including the *"imposter syndrome"* in what he dubbed the *"Freudian breakthrough"*. She gets over another fear, which is that of *high expectations*, where she didn't like disappointing the people who had placed their faith in her. Together they set goals and exercise visualization through the planning of different gameplay scenarios where confidence projection and maintaining stability under pressure were vital. She learned how to *"embody cognition"*, which meant that by embracing the feeling that she was desirous of, the body and mind would conjecture it in reality.

After incorporating Jared's and Erik's recommendations, Maria manages to regain her emotional stability as she was able to find time to recharge. She could now think straight, being mindful of the fact that *"time-pressure"* is a hindrance to proper decision making. She no longer felt displaced, whether in Vegas, New Jersey, or anywhere else. She gets cash from the European Poker Tour in Barcelona (109th for €3,790). She can even feel that she is thinking and playing better. There is no time pressure, and she is more proactive than before. She confesses that a revitalized sense of purpose to make the journey worthwhile has also enveloped her. She is second at Turbo in Dublin at the PokerStars Festival. She has some patience to take in invectives. Another second-place finish in Las Vegas for $6000. She is not judgemental when she is twentieth in EPT in Prague. It was to her, an impressive result considering her prior forays. Her confidence had genuinely grown, and she positively looked forward to the PCA.

CHAPTER THIRTEEN – GLORY DAYS: The Bahamas, January 2018

"Glory days" marks the third last chapter, and it is the culmination of her poker career. It illustrates how all the training she has undertaken in the past has molded her as a player. Through experience and rigorous learning, she acquired the skills to thrive in one of the most prestigious events in poker tournaments. She had clocked one year in her training and wanted to see how far she had gotten by playing at the PokerStars Caribbean Adventure (PCA). Although she busts out in her first attempt at the PCA – National Championship, she gets another opportunity at playing a turbo, which took sixteen hours of play.

She made it to the final table with only eight players remaining. Her progress was down to her *"mastery"* and *"chance"*. She was before intimidating opponents. Harrison Gimbel had a WSOP bracelet having won the *Crown of Poker* thrice, an EPT, and a *World Poker Tour* (WPT) title. Loek Van Wely, a chess champion in Holland, known as the *"Grandmaster"*. Chris Moorman, the player she dreaded most, was an opponent. Also, at the table were some pros from Canada and Chicago. She felt like an impostor before them but tried to collect herself after remembering Jared's advice, "They also have weaknesses because they are human *first* before they are players." In the way of a tip, her coach tells her not to be a *"fish"*.

Her overconfidence in her aces causes her to lose one-third of her stacks to the *"Grandmaster"*. He beats her to the river on a flopped straight. She wished she had realized that Loek must have had good hands when he raised a sizeable amount, but it was too late for her. Erik knows that she had screwed up but advises her to *"reset"* her mind and focus on playing the next hands, *"a hand at a time"*. Although she is down, she resets her mind after remembering the *"bird by bird"* strategy by Anne Lamott in her book, where a big project on birds was achieved *"bird by bird"*. Even when her chips reduce in size, she keeps her patience. Here you can learn that the state of mind and your focus matters.

Another section indicates the importance of having a routine, especially one that can help you declutter and make your mind fresh. Maria went through a routine that Jared had developed for her. It helped her to relax and freshen her mind. "Do you have a routine that helps you to decompress?"

When they resume the play, she dethrones a Brazilian player who busts out at position seven, following Chris Moorman, who was eighth. She appreciates that her mental discipline has somehow matured. Even with about twenty blinds, she is patient and wisely picks out her spots. She finds herself against an aggressive old player with the potential to lose a third of her chips. When she is about to quit by folding, she recalls the advice by Phil Galfond. He had told her always to be a *"detective"* and a *"storyteller"*. She needed to analyze the narrative and point out the *"inconsistencies"*. Maria did precisely that and evaluated the behavior of the *"Aggro oldie"*, the name she referred to him in her mind. She detects the logical gaps and uses it to deliver a big blow to her opponent. The author wins the pot when *"Aggro oldie"* reveals an ace-high that was not even paired against hers, which was paired. As she racks up her stacks, Harrison Gimbel is edged out by the *"Grandmaster"*.

Since Maria is famished, she discards her usual routine and decides to grab an energy bar and a cup of tea to fuel the brain. In the past, she has apprised that hunger can trigger *"negative"* emotional reactions that hamper decision making. Soon afterward, with two sevens, she faces the *"Grandmaster"* with what she calls *"Twelve Blinds"* and a *"Big dream"*. We all get to a point where we are at a disadvantaged position, but a moment occurs when we are availed with an opportunity to reach our dreams. That was her moment of dream-reaching. The flopped cards are six, eight, and nine. The turn is a ten. In a moment of what she believed was *"pure luck"*, she has the better hand and wins by a straight. The *"Grandmaster"* is no more. They became three after *"Grandmaster"* finishes in fourth place. Next, she edges out *"Aggro oldie"* with a straight. She is left only with a *"heads up"* match with the only other remaining opponent, Alexander Ziskin – the pro from Chicago. She knows that head-to-head calls for a different level of skills. She is not the one to make the mistake she did in Dublin when she played against the inebriated Swede. This time she believes she has packed the *"necessary skills"*. In the heads up against Alexander, the flop produces "Two tens and a seven with two spades." Alexander checks, the author bets, and the opponent raises her bet thrice. After thinking about why he raised, she calls the raise. After seeing a deuce of spades on the turn, Alexander decides to go all in. Maria contemplates, and her thinking tells her that she was the one likely to have better maths. She sensed that since she was an amateur, Alexander had a high probability of attempting a bluff. The *"amateur"* decides to call. Her flush draw beats a gunshot straight draw, which meant that he only had one card to make a straight. A king of hearts from the river is the card that confirms to her that she has won. Unbelievable to her, she won $84,600 and was declared the PCA National Champion for 2018.

As the chapter concludes, the author is happy that she has proven to herself that with the right tools and the right mindset and despite the challenges, *"chance"* can be *"conquered"*. However, it is not clear to her whether indeed she won out of *"luck"* or through her *"skills"*. She was worried about whether her success could be sustainable. Being the curious cat that she was, Maria was determined to study how the ratio of *"pluck"* and *"luck"* would pan out for her when she confronts the goddess of luck.

CHAPTER FOURTEEN – THE HEART OF THE GAMBLING BEAST: Macau, March 2018

The chapter starts with the author confessing that she has a nagging feeling. She can't quite say how skillful she has become. She is unsure whether she won the PCA out of luck or that her skill had something to do with it. "Are you afraid of being a one-hit-wonder? Have you ever felt like a fraud even after winning a competition?" In this chapter, Maria is determined to find out if she was *"skillful enough"* to triumph over *"luck"*. She has to know if she can keep her success going. Her victory at the PCA has brought with it attention from all spheres of life, and in her newfound glory, she is offered a formal sponsorship by Pokerstars to compete in Macau as a pro player.

Kevin, the founder of *Area/Code,* became a millionaire but felt *"undeserving"* of the millions because the *"unexpected windfall"* to him, was the work of nothing but *"luck"*. He was not sure either whether he earned it or luck had earned him the millions. Like Kevin, Maria had the same question when it came to her skills in poker.

Macau presents the ideal challenge for her to assess her skills. She is surprised that Macau is nothing like Las Vegas. She finds what she dreads most — *"gambling"* and according to her *"real gambling"* in Macau and not poker at the high-level she expected. As she experiences Macau, the author refers to it as the *"Belly of the Beast"* with ugliness unseen in other parts of the poker world. She mentions that Macau will drain your energy levels for all else except for that of gambling.

The chapter also takes a critical look into the idea of superstitions, which was conspicuous in Macau. The concept of lucky numbers, lucky colors, lucky outfits e.t.c are enshrined. Red is a *"lucky color", and* number eight is a *"lucky number"*. She is also startled that even great poker players with great mathematical ability and logical minds like Ike Haxton cultivate some form of superstition. "Wasn't it unhealthy to equate objects to mental wellness? Was a certain degree of control lost to such superstitions?" she wondered. From research in

Italy, the students who sat their exams on the seat with numbers considered culturally *"lucky"* were found to be *"overconfident"* even when the evidence stated otherwise.

Through other examples that she gives, she deduces that the brain is *"powerful"*. Our performance also will largely be dictated by our mental state. She warns that superstition can provide a sense of *"false confidence"* and as a downside, it can disturb your *"mental balance"* (equilibrium). Learning can be impeded because such superstitions are a deception of our abilities. "What happens when you lose your lucky object?" According to the author, you will also lose some degree of your mental equilibrium since a force beyond you has interfered with the object you associated with *"power"*.

"Why do you choose the irrational course even when you are fully aware that the alternative rational one is the "best"? This form of thinking, according to psychologist Jane Risen is a form of *"acquiescence"*. The author gives the example of Paul Magriel, aka X, who was mathematically gifted and became rich in playing backgammon but later on crushed down due to gambling and drug addiction. He was fully aware that unlike backgammon or poker, the outcomes of the table games which he played were *"uncontrollable"* (uncertain). He, however, played them because it gave him joy.

Gambling exploited *"weaknesses"* unlike poker, which involved *"precision"* and *"rewarded"* rationale. To the author, a believer of superstition was an outright *"gambler"*.

The author has come to appreciate the power that a *"belief"* can hold. Since how you feel affects how you act, Maria admits that confidence can translate to hot streaks even with the reality of a *"Gambler's fallacy"*. Perceived confidence, she adds, can make your opponent fold more in poker due to *"incorrect assumptions"*.

The author goes on to describe her strings of victories. She made two final tables at Macau and won $60,000. She also cashes in at the World Series *Main Event* by executing her best strategies. Maria clutches third place (€9,200) at the European Poker Tour out of over 1500 entries. She also clinches the twentieth spot at WBT Borgata out of 1,075 entries, getting almost $25,000, which is better than her salary during her first year at NYC. From her performances, the author can answer the very question she had at the beginning of the chapter. She accepts that she had acquired *"some skill"* and has overcome the obstruction of *"simple luck"*.

Maria becomes a finalist at the Global Poker Index awards and ends 2018 as one of the top five female players in poker tournaments. Although 2019 is not a stellar year for her, she can think through a decision without her ego getting the best of her. She has what she calls *"moments of simple beauty"*. Her own experience caused her husband to leave his lucrative job to start his own business. Her grandma is happy that her poker journey brought with it something that made her proud of Maria – the presentation she made in Davos at the World Economic Forum. There, she spoke of the association between poker and decision making.

CHAPTER FIFTEEN – LUDIC FALLACY: Las Vegas, June 2019

This chapter serves as an example of how the author applies the lessons from gaming in life. According to her, Nassib Taleb, author and statistician, had postulated that it would be impossible to perfectly apply the rules derived from games due to the *"sophisticated"* nature of life. He dismissed games as being *"simplistic"*. However, Maria reassures that it was the *"uncertainty"* in life that motivated her to embark on a project to discover if that was the case.

The author asserts that she has become *"calculative"* in terms of the mathematical and has *"emotional forbearance"*. She explained that even as they played, life happened. Through it all, the terrorist attack in Barcelona and the earthquakes that affected the WSOP tournaments. They gained more perspective and developed not only strength but *"survival skills"* to emerge as conquerors. Even as she finds herself playing at the table, she knows that she is very lucky. She quotes Richard Dawkins - "Most people are never going to die because they are never going to be born." Maria indicates that we find ourselves the winners of the *"lottery of life"*. Having been born when many, more deserving than us, the likes of better scientists than Isaac Newton or poets who would by far outsmart Keats, remain unborn. Out of chance, we are the ones who end up playing at the table. She states that "There is no skill in birth nor death, and in-between is the domain of luck." The author emphasizes that *"Chance is chance"*. It can't be controlled, and neither is it *"bad, good or personal"*. She paints it from the perspective of Epictetus, a Stoic philosopher. Epictetus relayed that the things *"born out of our actions"* e.g. pursuit or desire, we can control, but those *"beyond our actions"* e.g. body or reputation, will remain uncontrollable.

Perhaps one fabulous example of how lessons from gaming could be applied to real-life is when the author had an emergency after having an episode in her bathroom. In the hospital, while undergoing an MRI, she manages to remain *calm* for an entire two hours while under a tube. Her doctor is baffled that she was conscious the whole time. The author had spent the time in a moment of reflection, and just like a Stoic, she acknowledged what she could "*control*" and accepted that which was "*outside*" her "*control*". She was aware that how she could control her thoughts, decision processes, and reactions were what only mattered. Maria was stupefied at how composed she was and divulged that she would never have demonstrated such a level of calmness had the incidence occurred two years prior. It made her realize that she was finally embracing "*uncertainty*". The doctor's results reported that she had an intense migraine and not a stroke, as she'd thought.

While addressing uncertainty in life, the author uses the words of Carl Sagan that to understand the world, superstitions with its irrationality and false belief, science must be pursued. It can be best analyzed using the "*tools of rationality*" to investigate the "*unknown*". He elaborated that those who were afraid and assumed the knowledge of non-existent and control were more inclined towards superstitions. On the other hand, he said that the future belonged to those with the courage to explore the cosmos, even when their findings don't conform to their desires or viewpoints. To change the future, Sagan instructed that one must be able to learn, change, and accommodate the cosmos.

As the author concludes, *"life is not all skills"*. Skill only enables us to perceive the chances that the less-skilled or less-observant miss out on. She announces the *"biggest bluff"* - that in the moments that luck is not on our side, skills are *"ever enough"* to see us through to the next level. Many people view poker as a way of getting wealthy. Although she never got millions, the author reveals that the skills she amassed from the game, such as self-knowledge, decision making, and emotional strength are her truest wealth.

Background Information about the Biggest Bluff

The book details a personal quest by the author, where she dives head-on into the world of poker to investigate how skill and chance played out. She wanted to grasp the knowledge of how human beings could better understand the influence of luck and skill and use such knowledge to make improvements in their decision-making processes. It is a journey where she starts as a novice, progresses through critical and tough experiences. With zest and admirable determination, the author finally achieves proficiency in the game of poker. The epiphanies that the author draws from this odyssey that not only causes her to progress in her poker mastery but also motivates significant improvements in her own life.

The book is divided into three different parts. Part 1 is about the events in her life that led her to choose the game of poker for her experiment to investigate the impact of variance and skill. She narrates the start of her journey from her interactions with Erik Siedel, to her first lessons and eventually to playing poker online. Part 2 shows how the author makes progress from an amateur to the pro that she eventually becomes. It depicts the challenges she had to conquer until she achieved proficiency in poker. Part 3 takes place after she has won the 2018 PCA-National Championship. The section serves as an extended version of her experiment on skill and chance to prove to herself whether her success would be sustainable. "Was she capable of maintaining a long-lasting success?" It is also at this stage that the author, through an unfortunate incident in life, directs the reader to gain knowledge of how luck can be tamed.

This book provides a package of rich lessons to draw from that we can apply in our own individual lives. The book will accord us with strategies to boldly face and persevere through the biggest blows of life and still emerge on the other side as victors and not victims.

Background Information about Maria Konnikova

Maria Konnikova is a psychologist and a New York Times Best-selling author for her work in The Confidence Game (2016) and Mastermind (2013). Her latest work is The Biggest Bluff - How I learned to pay attention, master myself, and win (2020). She is a regular writer, contributing articles for The New Yorker and has written for The New York Times, The Atlantic, The Paris Review, The New Republic, The Boston Globe, Slate, The Wall Street Journal, Wired, Salon among others. She is a host at Grift, a podcast by Panoply Media, and also appears on another podcast, Gist, where she has her own segment.

Maria was born to Jewish parents in 1984 in Moscow, Russia, but her family immigrated to the U.S. when she was four years old. She did her B.A. in Psychology with creative writing at Harvard University and her Ph.D. in Psychology from Columbia University under the tutelage of psychologist Walter Mischel.

Maria is also an international poker champion, having been trained by Erik Siedel, a poker champion. She has earned over $300,000 from her poker tournaments.

Through her writing, she has won numerous awards, and she continues to contribute to the science of psychology through her writings on the subject of human behavior.

Awards and Accolades

- 2019 Excellence in Science Journalism Award from the Society of Personality and Social Psychology

- 2019 National Magazine Award nomination

- PokerStars Caribbean Adventures (PCA) – National Champion for 2018

- Winner of the 2016 Robert P. Balles Prize in Critical Thinking – *The Confidence Game*

- Winner of the Best American Science and Nature Writing - *Altered Tastes,* an article about Heston Blumenthal. The article was translated into more than twenty languages.

- Award nomination for Best Nonfiction - *Mastermind: How to Think Like Sherlock Holmes*

Cover Questions

- What is the main idea of *The Biggest Bluff*?

- How does poker contribute to the narrative of gender inclusivity?

- Why is poker considered the embodiment of the American dream?

- Why are modern games *"imperfectly"* designed?

- Why is *"betting"* integral to the learning process?

- Why is the dragonfly theory important in the art of playing poker?

Trivia Questions about The Biggest Bluff

- What question does Phil Galfond urge her always to ask herself when an opponent made a move?

- What are the full names of the author's coach?

- Which part of our brain, based on the visual system, is responsible for rapid judgment?

- Which style of play in poker is synonymous with older people?

- State any two recommendations by Blake Eastman on how the author can improve her game.

- Which syndrome did the author eliminate through the help of Jared Tendler?

- Which position did the author finish in when she played the Turbo event in Dublin?

- At the final table of the PCA – National Championship, which player did the author fear most?

- The advice of *"Bird by Bird"* was from a book that was written by which author?

- Which color in Macau is associated with luck?

- How much money did the author win at the PCA tournament?

- In the final chapter, what skills does the author refer to as her truest wealth?

- Which famous scientist motivated the author to learn poker?

- Which event does the author mention as the *World cup, the Masters, the Super-Bowl"* in the world of Poker?

- Which player does the author refer to as the *"incarnation of focus"*?

Trivia Questions about Maria Konnikova

- Where was the author born?

- At what age did her family immigrate to the United States?

- Which university did the author attend for her undergraduate studies?

- Which prominent psychologist guided the author in her Ph.D. research?

- How much in total did the author earn from her poker tournaments?

Discussion Questions

- How does the concept of *"irrational perseverance"* promotes failure?

- Discuss how *"time-pressure"* can affect decision-making

- Is Slepian research similar to the *"Beyond Tells"* research by Eastman?

- Why should we be careful when we receive *"participation trophies"* instead of a podium finish?

- Why do people overestimate what they can achieve in one year and underestimate what they can achieve in ten years?

- Why does the author choose *No Limit Texas Hold'em* to learn poker even when there are other variations of poker?

Thank You!

Hope you've enjoyed your reading experience.

We here at Rapid Reads will always strive to deliver to you the highest quality guides.

So I'd like to thank you for supporting us and reading until the very end.

Before you go, would you mind leaving us a review on Amazon?

It will mean a lot to us and support us creating high quality guides for you in the future.

Thanks once again and here's where you can leave a review.

Warmly yours,

The Spark Reads Team

Printed in Great Britain
by Amazon

45329614R00059